# NEUES PALAIS
# IN SANSSOUCI

# NEUES PALAIS IN SANSSOUCI

FOTOGRAFIEN VON | PHOTOGRAPHS BY
FRIEDERIKE VON RAUCH

BETRACHTET VON | CONTEMPLATED BY
RUDOLF PRINZ ZUR LIPPE

HERAUSGEGEBEN VON DER | EDITED BY
GENERALDIREKTION DER
STIFTUNG PREUSSISCHE SCHLÖSSER
UND GÄRTEN BERLIN-BRANDENBURG

jovis

STIFTUNG
PREUSSISCHE SCHLÖSSER UND GÄRTEN
BERLIN-BRANDENBURG

## ZUR EINLEITUNG: DAS NEUE PALAIS IM WANDEL

Samuel Wittwer

Das Neue Palais im Garten von Sanssouci wurde von 1765 bis 1768 im Auftrag Friedrichs des Großen errichtet. Bereits vor dem Siebenjährigen Krieg (1756–1763) hatte er Planungen zu einem größeren Schlossbau aufgenommen. Nun, als Sieger in die erste Reihe europäischer Potentaten aufgestiegen, wurde der Bau mit allen erdenklichen Mitteln in einer solchen Prächtigkeit ausgeführt, dass der König ihn selbst als eine „Fanfaronnade", eine Prahlerei, bezeichnete. In diesem Schloss, das ähnlich einem Hotel lediglich aus Gästeappartements, Festsälen und einem Theater bestand, versammelte er fortan während eines Monats im Jahr Teile der weit verzweigten Familie sowie Freunde zu glanzvollen Festen.

Die Bedeutung als Ort des geselligen Beisammenseins behielt das Neue Palais auch für die nachfolgenden Generationen der Hohenzollern bei, wenngleich das Schloss deutlich weniger genutzt wurde. Das änderte sich erst in der zweiten Hälfte des 19. Jahrhunderts, als Kronprinz Friedrich (III.) und seine Gattin Victoria hier eine Sommerresidenz einrichteten. Für ihren Sohn Wilhelm (II.) und seine Frau Auguste Victoria wurde das Schloss nach der Thronbesteigung 1888 sogar zur eigentlichen privaten Hauptresidenz. Beide Generationen bauten das Palais für die umfangreiche Hofhaltung kontinuierlich aus und um Neue Räume, Durchwegungen und Möblierungen wurden geschaffen. Bei allen Neugestaltungen, ja selbst bei Einbauten nach neuester Technik wurde darauf geachtet, den Stil des späten friderizianischen Rokokos beizubehalten. Dieses „Weiterbauen an Geschichte" brach 1918 mit der Revolution und dem Exil der kaiserlichen Familie zunächst ab. Das Schloss verlor seine Doppelfunktion als privater Wohnsitz und dynastischer Repräsentationsort. Mit der Übernahme durch den Staat und der Öffnung als Museum wurde es zum Denkmal. Die Ausstattung wurde dazu auf Basis historischer Inventare sorgfältig re-friderizianisiert, nur wenige Elemente erinnerten noch direkt an die Nutzung durch Wilhelm II. Diese Rückgewinnung des Gesamtkunstwerks Friedrichs des Großen schien den Verantwortlichen jener Zeit die einzige Möglichkeit im Umgang mit der Geschichte des Hauses. Eine Zäsur brachten der Zweite Weltkrieg und seine Folgen mit sich, das heißt den Verlust von bedeutenden Teilen der Erstausstattung des 18. Jahrhunderts. Dies zwang – und zwingt – die Museumsleute bis heute, kreative Lösungen dort zu entwickeln, wo eine Annäherung an die historischen Inventare nicht mehr mit originalen Stücken möglich ist. Obwohl die Denkmalidee einen bestimmten Zustand erhalten und vermitteln möchte, müssen immer wieder Anpassungen an ein sich veränderndes Besucherverhalten, andere Schwerpunkte der Vermittlungsinhalte oder technische Neuerungen vorgenommen werden; so etwa beim Wegfall der klassischen Glühbirne, als es darum ging, einen Ersatz zu finden, der der kaiserzeitlichen Lichtqualität der frühen Elektrifizierung nahekommt.

Aber: Was kümmert dies das Schloss? Es hat hingenommen, dass in der Nachkriegszeit aus Platznot immer mehr Funktionen der wachsenden Schlösserverwaltung Einzug hielten, dass Restaurierungsateliers eingerichtet, die Graphische Sammlung hierhergebracht oder die Depotverwaltung gegründet wurde. Es hat sich mit den Geheimnissen seiner Fluchten

# BY WAY OF AN INTRODUCTION: THE NEW PALACE ON THE TIDE OF CHANGE

Samuel Wittwer

The New Palace in the garden of Sanssouci was built at the behest of Frederick the Great between 1765 and 1768. Even before the Seven Years War (1756–1763) he had made a start on a palatial building project. After gaining a place in the front rank of European rulers as one of the war's victors, he invested all available means in completing the building, doing so with such magnificence that he himself dubbed it a 'Fanfaronnade' – 'sheer boasting', 'blowing his own trumpet'. At this palace, which rather like a hotel consisted solely of guest apartments, halls and a theatre, he took to bringing parts of his extensive broader family together for one month in the year, along with friends, for a series of sparkling festivities.

Under the following generations of Hohenzollerns, the New Palace retained its importance as a location for social gatherings, though they did not use it as much as Frederick the Great had. Nor was this to change until the second half of the nineteenth century, when Crown Prince Friedrich (III) and his consort Victoria built a summer residence there. After he came to the throne in 1888, the palace even became the principal private residence of their son Wilhelm (II) and his consort Auguste Victoria. Both generations continually adapted and extended the palace for their court households. New rooms, passages and sets of furnishings were created. In all these undertakings, care was constantly taken to adhere to the late Friderician Rococo style, even when the adaptations involved technical innovations. Following the imperial family's withdrawal into exile at the November Revolution of 1918, the practice of faithfulness to their great forebear's historical manner came to an end and the palace lost its double function of private residence and locus of dynastic representation. Taken over by the state and opened up as a museum, it now became a historical monument. Furthermore, the furnishings were painstakingly 're-Fridericianized' on the basis of historical inventories, so that only a few elements remained to testify to the use of the palace by Kaiser Wilhelm II. To those responsible at the time, the restoration of Frederick the Great's *Gesamtkunstwerk* seemed to be the only justifiable way of handling the palace's particular history. A further turning point came with the Second World War, when the palace lost considerable parts of its original eighteenth-century furnishings. This forced – and continues to force – the museum's curators to find creative solutions in cases where it is no longer possible to reflect the historical inventories with absolute authenticity. Although the principle of the 'historical monument' makes it an imperative to preserve a given building in a certain state and interpret it for its visitors, changes in the public's habits and behaviour mean that presentation has to be constantly adapted, as do the focuses of media and education work. This also applies to technical innovations, one example being the problem of how to respond to the disappearance of the classical light bulb, which has had to be replaced with light sources approximating to the light quality obtaining at the early installation of electricity in imperial times.

But what does all that matter to the New Palace itself? It coped with the developments of the post-war period, when the lack of space elsewhere for the ever-increasing functions of the Prussian Palaces and Gardens resulted in it being used to accommodate restoration workshops,

und Winkel, seinen Dekorationen und dem besonderen Geruch behauptet, als Bereiche neben den Museumsräumen zu Arbeitsplätzen und diese vielen Mitarbeitern wiederum zu einer vertrauten Umgebung wurden. Dabei waren die Rahmenbedingungen hierfür nicht besonders bequem, denn viele Treppen, Kälte und Dunkelheit ließen kaum Gedanken an ein romantisches Leben im Schloss aufkommen. Und doch bildete sich ein von Nostalgie geprägter Stolz aus, unmittelbar am historischen Ort für eben diesen Kosmos an Kunst und Geschichte tätig sein zu dürfen.

Das ist es, was man als die besondere Atmosphäre des Neuen Palais bezeichnen könnte: ein Haus, das sich widersetzt, einfach nur Museum oder nur Arbeitsplatz oder nur Geschichtskapsel zu sein. Auf der einen Seite „eingefrorene" Prachträume, in denen jedes Detail Bedeutung ausdrückt, beachtet und betrachtet werden will; auf der anderen Seite Räume, die den Rahmen für alltägliche Arbeitsgänge bilden und denen man mit von Respekt getragener, routinemäßiger Selbstverständlichkeit begegnet. Oder begegnete. Denn nun wird dem Schloss jene Intensiv-Pflegekur zuteil, auf die es seit fast hundert Jahren wartet. Seine Dächer werden saniert, die Fenster aufgearbeitet, Keller und Sockel dringend notwendigen Ertüchtigungen unterworfen, und die Fremdnutzungen, die nicht nur romantisch, sondern auch belastend waren, ziehen aus. Auch stehen in den kommenden Jahren immer wieder behutsame Restaurierungen in den Innenräumen an. Dies alles wird das Palais verändern, und auch wenn sein eigenwilliger Charme stärker ist als alle Eingriffe, so wird es nach Jahrzehnten der Verträumtheit einmal mehr in seiner Geschichte ein neues Gesicht bekommen.

Die leichte Wehmut, dieser Hauch von Nostalgie, die hier mitschwingt, brachte letztlich den Wunsch auf, ein kleines Bisschen von dieser Stimmung festzuhalten zu versuchen. Nicht dokumentarisch, aber künstlerisch musste es doch gelingen, das „intime Leben im Neuen Palais", wie Rudolf zur Lippe es treffend nannte, einzufangen. Sensibilität war gefragt, aber auch jemand, der ein „positives Verhältnis zu Staub" hat, Patina von Dreck unterscheiden kann und die Stille liebt. Die Berliner Künstlerin Friederike von Rauch ist so jemand. Seit nunmehr sieben Jahren hat sie in diesem Projekt die Möglichkeit, sich jederzeit frei im Neuen Palais zu bewegen, allein mit ihrer Kamera. In unzähligen dieser Zwiegespräche mit dem Schloss lernten sie einander kennen, entstanden Aufnahmen, in denen man die emotionale Vertrautheit der beiden spürt. Es sind komische Momente dabei, aber auch besinnliche, stille Begegnungen ebenso wie laute. Das entstandene Porträt zeigt das Schloss nicht im Festtagskleid, sondern so, wie es alle die erleben dürfen, die hier im Alltag tätig sind und waren. Und es spiegelt die ungeheure Würde dieses Hauses wider.

Eine der ersten Reaktionen auf diesen besonderen Blick auf nur vermeintlich Bekanntes sind die wunderbaren Gedankenspiele der Texte von Rudolf zur Lippe. Der Philosoph und Ästhetiker lädt den Leser ein, sich für die kleinen Absurditäten, die einigen Bildern eigen sind, zu sensibilisieren. Er beschreibt, assoziiert und öffnet Augen, ohne den Motiven ihr Geheimnis zu nehmen. Entstanden ist eine Charakterstudie, die die stillen Herrlichkeiten dieses Schlosses zum Ausdruck bringt, jenseits von Marmor, Gold und Spiegelung.

the collection of prints and drawings, and the office newly founded to administer the collections' depositories. With all its secret passageways and nooks and crannies, its interior decoration and its characteristic smell, it held its own when areas adjacent to the museum rooms became working rooms. In their turn, these became a familiar environment for the many staff who came to work at the palace, in conditions that were far from comfortable, with the many staircases, the cold and the darkness hardly being conducive to thoughts of life there ever having been romantic. And yet the staff concerned developed a certain nostalgic pride and a sense of being privileged to be working at this historic location for the advancement of this particular cosmos of art and history.

That, in a nutshell, is what the special atmosphere of the New Palace is all about. A house that refuses to be just a museum, or just a place of work, or just a time-warp. On the one hand, 'deep-frozen' state rooms with masses of significant details wanting us to take time to consider and contemplate them; on the other hand, rooms that are the scene of everyday working procedures that we have come to take for granted but nevertheless regard with a profound respect. Or, I should say, regarded. For the palace is now being treated to the programme of intensive care for which it has been waiting for almost a hundred years. Its roofs are being refurbished and its windows restored, and the cellar and basement storey are being subjected to urgently required structural work. And the third-party usages, which may have been romantic but also took their toll on the palace, are coming to an end. In addition, the coming years will see a succession of restoration projects being carried out on the interiors. All this will change the palace, and even though its idiosyncratic charm may be stronger than all the encroachments it has suffered, it will – now that its decades of dreamy slumber are over – acquire a new face, just as it so often has in the past.

Finally, the slight wistfulness and nostalgia that resonate in the above paragraph generated the desire to try to preserve a little of this special atmosphere. But if what Rudolf zur Lippe has aptly called the 'intimate life in the New Palace' was to be captured for posterity, that could evidently only be done by artistic, and not documentary, means. What the project needed was not only sensitivity but also someone with a 'positive relationship with dust', someone capable of distinguishing patina from dirt and someone with a love of silence. The Berlin artist Friederike von Rauch is just such a person. For seven years she was free to go anywhere she wished in the palace, alone with her camera. In innumerable dialogues she and the palace got to know each other and she took photographs in which one can sense their mutual emotional familiarity. They contain amusing moments but there are also more serious encounters, some tranquilly contemplative and others loud. The portrait that has resulted does not show the palace in its Sunday best but, rather, as those who have worked here have been fortunate enough to experience it. And it is a portrait that reflects the palace's enormous dignity.

Amongst the first reactions to this special view of a world we think we know so well have been the wonderful thought-play texts from the pen of the philosopher and aesthetician Rudolf zur Lippe, who invites his readers to sensitize themselves to the little absurdities inherent in some of the pictures. What he has written is a character study that pays due tribute to the quiet glories of this palace, far beyond its marble, its gold, and its mirrors.

# PETITES PERCEPTIONS

Rudolf Prinz zur Lippe

Schlösser leben – selbstverständlich – anders. Sie wurden erbaut als Residenzen, manchmal als Musenhöfe oder Jagdrelais. Manche wurden zu Lustschlössern ernannt. Und doch wurden die meisten erst einmal auch als Wohnsitz geschaffen. Zumindest stellen wir uns vor, dass dies ihre gewöhnliche Aufgabe sei. Nicht nur die Kinder heutiger Besucher fragen, „wer wohnt denn da?". Friederike von Rauch ist Zeugin einer ganz anderen Existenz des Neuen Palais geworden in den Bedingungen eines Interregnums ohne Bestimmung und ohne Ende. Ihre Bilder sind in Ansätzen Blicke auf ein anderes Leben an diesem Ort. Nicht Dokumentation eines nun vergangenen Zustandes. Nicht Klage überwundenen Zerfalls oder zerstörter Idyllen, die auf immer beseitigt sind. Atmosphären wehen uns an, die zu dem Ort in alle Zukunft gehören werden, wie sie ihm, aus anderen oder ähnlichen Zuständen, seit je eigen geworden sind. Ein intimes Leben, das sich in die Falten der Interieurs zurückzieht, wenn die Wärter die Fensterläden öffnen, um das Greifbare und Schätzbare der Räume für die Besichtigungen in deutliches Licht setzen.
„Ich hatte versprochen, die Herzogin von Giovane zu besuchen, die auf dem Schloss wohnte, wo man mich dann viele Stufen hinauf durch manche Gänge wandern ließ, deren oberste verengt durch Kisten, Schränke und alles Missfällige eines Hofgarderobewesens waren." So gelangt Goethe in Neapel zu einer liebenswürdigen Gastgeberin. Er wundert sich durchaus über solch einen Gang durch ein Schloss. Was wir mit Friederike von Rauch erleben, ist aber nicht nur wunderlich. Es ist gar kein Gang. Es sind einzelne Szenen, von denen manche etwas mit dem gleichen Potsdamer Barock zu tun haben, andere nichts oder nur ganz am Rande. Diese beziehen dann ein Interesse daraus, dass wir wissen, sie haben im Neuen Palais existiert. Die Existenz aller Szenen lebt in der Spannung zu dem, was sie gegenwärtig nicht sind, ob sie nun von unerwarteten neuen Funktionen bestimmt sind oder in einem Nachleben der einstigen Bestimmungen dahindämmern. Manchmal auch darin aufgestört durch Eingriffe und Übergriffe aus einer anderen Realität. Kaum je ein Gang aus dem Einen in ein Anderes. Eher ein disparates Panoptikum.

Wenn die Läden und die Vorhänge die Räume verdunkeln, geben manchmal schöne Lichtquellen einen Schimmer von Helligkeit, wie zu einer heimlichen Verabredung. Deutlich nur an einer glänzenden Kante hier und da, die das Auge ertastet, in den Schimmer einer seidenglänzenden Wandbespannung hinein, entlang an Sessellehnen, bis sie auf das Dunkel einer Tischplatte treffen. Ein Türknauf sagt, dass es da einen Ausgang geben könnte. Unwillkürlich spürt die Nase einer Portiere nach, ob sie zu einer Fensternische mit ihrer frischeren Luft oder einem Alkoven gehört. Als Kindern war es uns gleich, weil beide gute Verstecke versprachen. Aber wir nannten sie den „Gespenstermops im Dustern", weil, so oder so, gerade die besten Verstecke nicht ganz geheuer sind. Je sicherer man sich vor denen, die suchen mussten, wissen konnte, desto tückischer lauerte immer auch die Gefahr, am Ende gar nicht mehr gefunden zu werden. Dieses Dunkel hat doch immer etwas Lauerndes, das aus den Ecken und hinter nur

# PETITES PERCEPTIONS

Rudolf Prinz zur Lippe

Grand country houses and town palaces live – it goes without saying – differently. Most were built as residences, though some were courts of the muses or hunting lodges. Some, even, were raised to the status of *maison de plaisance*. Yet the vast majority were first and foremost created to be lived in. At least this is what we imagine to be their usual purpose. 'Who lives in there?' is a question asked not only by the children of present-day visitors. Friederike von Rauch has been witness to the New Palace having a quite different existence, under a seemingly endless interregnum without any fixed purpose. Her pictures are to a certain extent visions of a different life at this place. Not some kind of documentation of a state now past. Not some statement about how decay has been overcome or a lament for idylls destroyed, never to be seen again. In them we sense atmospheres that will belong to the place for ever, just as they have belonged to it, as a result of it having been in different or similar states, since time immemorial. Atmospheres of an intimate life that retreats into the folds of the interior when the custodians open the shutters for forthcoming visitors, to bring the tangible and quantifiable into the clear light of day.

'I had promised to visit the Duchess of Giovane, who lived at the castle. There I was led up many stairs and along a number of corridors, the topmost of which was cluttered with chests, cupboards and all the unpleasant aspects of a court wardrobe.' This was how Goethe made his way to an amiable hostess in Naples. Having to take such a path through a castle clearly set him wondering. While what we experience with Friederike von Rauch is also wondrous, it is not a path. It consists of individual scenes, some of which have a certain amount to do with the same *Potsdamer Barock* and some nothing, or only tangentially. The latter scenes are interesting because we know that they existed at the New Palace. All the scenes have a certain vibrancy by virtue of what they are at present not, whether they are now characterized by unexpected new functions or just slumbering on in the after-life of their former identities, occasionally being aroused by interventions and assaults from another reality. Hardly ever do we see a path from one space to another. What we see is, rather, a disparate panopticon.

When the rooms are darkened by the shutters and curtains, bright gleams are sometimes emitted by beautiful light sources, as if for a secret rendezvous. They are only clearly visible on shining edges here and there, which the eye makes out by following them into the shimmer of a lustrous silk wall hanging or along the backs of chairs until they hit the darkness of a table top. Over there, a door knob tells us that there might be a way out. Instinctively, one looks more closely at a curtain hanging over a door to see whether it leads to a window niche and fresher air, or to an alcove. When we were children it was all the same to us, as both made good hiding places when we played what we called 'spooky hide-and-seek'. Actually we found all hiding places a bit frightening, especially the best ones, because the more we knew we were out of reach of the seekers, the greater was the danger that we might even not be found at all. For this kind of darkness always has something insidious about it, something lurking, waiting to steal forth

zu ahnenden Schränken hervorschleicht. Es erlaubt Mustern ein blasses Eigenleben als Vögel oder Blumen zu entfalten, an das wir anstoßen mit unserem Atem. Schlösser „ohne Leben" leben anders. Oft in Verwunderlichkeiten.

Als imaginären Flaneur durch das Neue Palais der Zwischenzeiten soll mich leiten, was Goethe in seiner Italienischen Reise als Einsicht von den Eindrücken sizilianischer Landschaften und Orte mitteilt: Dichter wie Homer stellten die Existenz dar, wir „gewöhnlichen" den Effekt; sie schilderten das Fürchterliche, wir schildern fürchterlich; sie schilderten das Angenehme, wir schildern angenehm usw. Dazu verpflichten schon die Fotografien von Friederike von Rauch, wie sie auch dazu einladen. Diese Bilder verpflichten dazu, weil sie sich nicht als Dokumentation missverstehen lassen. Sie weisen nicht auf Fakten hin. Sie laden ein, Situationen zu erleben, wie die Fotografin dort von diesen Momenten des Daseins angetroffen worden ist. Sie schlagen uns vor, zu erleben, wie sie leben. Goethe spricht von Existenz, wie Sartre sie für uns in seinem Essay „Venise de ma fenêtre" vergegenwärtigt. Nichts ist Faktum. Alles ist Konstellation. Alles ist, wie die Dinge sich und uns begegnen.

–

Zwischen zwei Fensterläden ein Spalt, fingerbreit und vom Boden bis hinauf. Unter den Flügeln der Tür eine Ritze, noch schmaler. Eine Tür ist es und daneben, im Winkel, eine Fensternische. Diese würde weiß sein, jene grün. Darauf schimmern breit und auf einigen Leisten schwärzlich enorme Vergoldungen. Wie über dem Türbogen Wülste und Schnörkel eines gewaltigen Ornaments. Oder ist es eine Szene, die diese doch eher schmale Prunktür krönt, wo eine gemalte Supraporte zu wenig hergemacht hätte? Wo sind wir? Kaum ein Raum, kaum eine Ecke, kaum Licht und Schatten. Wo das Regiment, kaum von diesen Kanten gestört, ein anonymes Dunkel führt, lassen Schatten nichts zurück und Beleuchtung nichts hervortreten. Diese Dunkelheit ist charakterlos. Erst hier wird einem bewusst, dass sie an anderen Orten etwas von einer, wenn auch nicht greifbaren, Stofflichkeit besitzt. So wie Nebel, wenn er so dicht ist, dass hinter dem Nebel, an den wir zu stoßen scheinen, nichts ist als mehr Nebel und mehr Nebel.

Dieses Dunkel hier ist stumpf. So langweilig ohne irgendeine Ahnung von Geheimnis. Dieses Gefühl bestätigt eine winzige metallene Angel der Tür. Man wird sich ihrer erst bewusst, da man wiederholt nach Anhaltspunkten sucht. Nun aber, endlich wichtig geworden, macht sie, kaum größer als ein polierter Nagel, erbarmungslos klar, alles eben noch, wenn auch mit Mühe Beschriebene erreicht nicht die Wirklichkeit.

Im Clair-obscur der wichtigsten Gemälde von Caravaggio leben Figuren und was ihnen begegnet zu einer höchst berührenden Transparenz auf, wie sie einst vergoldete Heiligenscheine treuherzig behauptet haben. Hier bleibt von Dunkel und Hell nur die traurige Präsenz ihres Grauwertes. Und auch das Gold, so massiv zum Einsatz gebracht, hat nichts mehr zu sagen. Manchmal hat eben solch einen Prunk definitiv sein Leben verlassen.

Ein Schein von Licht auf den silbrigen Profilen der Vertäfelung rechts und links rahmt das große finstere Loch. Nichts verrät, von wo er kommen mag. Gebrochenes Aufblinken von Ornamentleisten verrät nicht mehr. Doch muss jenes Licht eigentlich nicht zu schwach sein, so diffus es

from the corners or from behind wardrobes only vaguely intuited. It allows patterns to develop a dimly perceptible life of their own, as birds or flowers, that we collide into with our breath. Palaces that are 'un-lived-in' live differently. Often in wondrous ways.
As an imaginary *flâneur* in the New Palace of this interim period I am to be guided by the insight which Goethe, under the impression of Sicilian towns and landscapes, shares with us in his Italian Journey, namely, that while poets of the likes of Homer represented existence, we commonly represent the effect: they depicted the terrifying, we depict terrifyingly; they described the pleasurable, we describe pleasingly, and so on. The photographs of Friederike von Rauch invite us – and indeed make it our duty – to be guided by this insight. The pictures impose this obligation upon us because they do not allow themselves to be misunderstood as a documentary project. They do not point out facts. They invite us to experience situations just as the photographer was confronted with them. They invite us to experience how they live. Goethe speaks of existence as Sartre evokes existence for us in his essay 'Venise de ma fenêtre'. Nothing is fact. All is constellation. It all comes down to how things encounter one another and how things encounter us.

—

A gap no broader than a finger between two window shutters, from top to bottom. Down at floor level a chink, even slighter. It is a door, and next to it in the corner is a window niche. The latter would be white, the former green. On the door massive gilded elements shimmer expansively, some of the gilded profiles blackishly. Likewise, over the door, the protuberances and flourishes of a huge ornament. Or, rather, is this somewhat narrow state door perhaps crowned by a scene, because a painted sopraporta would have made too little of an effect? Where are we? Hardly a room, hardly a corner, hardly any light or shadows. Where an anonymous darkness holds sway, hardly disturbed by these gleaming surfaces, the shadows leave nothing behind and the lighting brings nothing out. This darkness is characterless. Only here does one become aware that in other places the darkness possesses a certain intangible materiality. Like fog when it is so thick that behind the fog that we seem to bump into there is nothing but fog and yet more fog.
The darkness here is dull. So dreary, without the slightest hint of mystery. This feeling is confirmed by a tiny metal door hinge that one only notices because one is incessantly searching for points of reference. But now, hardly larger than a polished nail but now finally important, the hinge makes it mercilessly clear: everything that has been described so far with such great effort does not come up to the reality.
In the chiaroscuro of Caravaggio's most important paintings, figures and what they encounter come to life in an extremely moving transparency, like the transparency that once shone forth so steadfastly from gilded haloes. Here, all that remains of light and dark is the sad presence of their greyness. Even the gold, laid on so thick, has nothing more to say. Sometimes, all the life has gone out of stateliness such as this.

The large dark cavity is framed to left and right by light shining on the silvery half-rounds of the panelling. Nothing tells us where the light is coming from. Gleams on ornamental mouldings here and there do not tell us much either. But the light cannot be so very weak, however diffusely it

sich auch immer noch auf seitlich gerafften Stoffen verfängt. Darinnen. Nicht bloß ein Loch in der Wand, vermutlich eines kunstvollen Zimmers. Nein, eine schwarze Tiefe ohne jede Gestalt oder Struktur. So tief, dass sie die Macht einer unauslotbaren Gegenwelt hat. Die Macht, unsere Welt aufzusaugen und aufzulösen. Nein, im Vordergrund verblasst Gold zu Silber. Die Düsternis zieht hervor wie Nebelschwaden und saugt die Farben auf.

Was wir immerhin deutlich genug erkennen, erscheint wie das Skelett eines Bettes mit den Schals eines Leichenhemdes. Aus jener Tiefe vorgeschoben wie das auch ihr Unverdauliche. Schatten auf Polstern wollten eigentlich alles verschlingen und sind nur am Gerippe hängen geblieben, als es uns ausgespuckt wurde. Sie gehören zu dem Dunkel, das dahinter Materie in eine Finsternis verwandelt. Die irgendwo beginnt, undurchdringlich zu werden. Man steht davor wie Ödipus am Ende seiner Irr- und Sühnefahrt vor der Höhle zur Unterwelt. Erlösung, doch ohne Wiederkehr. Späte Gnade, im Reich der Schatten. Den Lebenden lässt er nur einen Segen zurück, ohne zu ahnen, worin sie bestärkt werden können.

Diese Phantasmen ergreifen einen so zwingend, dass man vergisst, was ein Fremdenführer hier sagt, wenn er die Szene dem Tageslicht zurückgibt: „Das Bett von Friedrich dem Großen". Den sehen wir aber eher auf den Feldbetten seiner Kriegszüge als hier im Prunk während der Wochen im Sommerpalais. Oder am Fenster seiner Bibliothek in Sanssouci mit dem Blick hinüber zu seinem Grab auf der Terrasse, das er zugleich mit dem Grundstein dieses schlossweiten Pavillons ausheben ließ. Philosoph genug, um die Welt, in der goldene Betten etwas gelten, der Staffage zu überlassen.

Ist es nicht merkwürdig, keine der Szenen hat mich bis jetzt darauf gebracht, von ihrem Geruch zu sprechen. Nun sehe ich mich gegenüber einer Wand mit einer Hängung von Bildern unter weißen Verpackungen. Verschiedene Formate, dicht an dicht. Eine einfache Tür dazwischen steht offen. Sie gibt den Blick frei auf eine Reihe offenbar gleichartiger Räume. Er folgt den Türrahmen in fortgesetzter Folge. Von einer Enfilade wird man bei so bescheidenen Zimmern nicht sprechen. Allerdings, ein wenig gehoben ist ihr Status dennoch. Die Türen haben ihre abgesetzten Profile und leichte Bögen, dunkel umrandet, und die Wände Boiserien mit sogar ein wenig verblasstem Gold … Dunkle Dielen der Böden sind eben deutlich genug wahrzunehmen als ein solider Grund von alters her. Eben. Es zieht einem hier etwas entgegen wie jener penetrante Geruch von Karbolineum, der unmittelbar an öffentliche Gebäude der DDR erinnert. Mit Vorfahren, die auch im Westen der Nachkriegszeit die Stuben von Jugendherbergen beherrschten, dort mit dem Duft von Vierfruchtmarmelade abgestimmt.

Diese zugeklebt verpackten Bilder ziehen sich durch alle Räume, einer hinter dem anderen. Als einziges Mobiliar. Es ist wohl weniger dieser Fußboden an sich, dem der ominöse Hauch vom kategorischen Imperativ der Beamtenhygiene entströmt. Es muss auch diese penible Abwesenheit jeglichen Inhalts, eben von allem Sichtbaren sein, die ihn gleich mit suggeriert. Das war es, was mir so unverhofft bei meinem ersten Besuch im Ostberliner Amt der Denkmalpfleger entgegenschlug. Auf breiten Treppen und langen Gängen. Wo ähnlich das Tageslicht draußen warten musste. Sie waren allerdings einfach leer, als ob es dort um nichts ginge. Nichts als diesen Geruch?

Und hier? Geht es um etwas? Diese blanken Papiere sprechen von nichts. Das sind keine Verhüllungen, wie Christo sie liebevoll etwas für ihn Besonderem widmet. Die vermutlich früher

gets caught in the fabrics gathered to the sides. In there. Not just a hole in the wall of what is most likely an exquisitely decorated room. No, a black deepness without any form or structure. So deep that it has the power of an unfathomable counter-world. The power to suck in and dissolve our world. No, in the foreground, gold pales to silver. The gloom advances like swathes of fog and swallows up the colours.

Fairly clearly recognizable, however, is something like the skeleton of a bed decked out with lengths of burial shroud. Shoved forward as if having proved indigestible to the depths from which it came. As if the shadows on the upholstery had wanted to swallow everything but got stuck on the carcass when it was spewed out at us. They belong to the gloom behind, which transforms matter into sheer darkness. And at some point the darkness begins to become impenetrable. One stands in front of it like Oedipus at the end of his pilgrimage of atonement in front of the cave leading to the underworld. Redemption, but without return. Late grace, in the realm of the shades. All he leaves for the living is a blessing, without knowing what it is they are to be strengthened in.

These phantasms hold us so compellingly captive that we become oblivious to what the tour guides say when putting the scene back into the light of day: 'Frederick the Great's bed'. We for our part tend to see him on the camp beds of his military campaigns rather than here in splendour during his summer palace weeks. Or at the window of his library at Sanssouci, looking over to his burial place on the terrace, the grave that he had dug when the foundation stone of this schloss-sized pavilion was laid. Philosopher enough almost to disregard a world that sets such store by golden beds.

Isn't it strange, none of the scenes so far has prompted me to talk of its smell. Now I find myself confronted by a wall hung with pictures all wrapped in white. Various sizes, densely arranged. A single door stands open, allowing one to look through to a series of rooms that are clearly all of the same kind. The eye follows the regular sequence of receding door frames. While such modest rooms could hardly be described as an enfilade, they nevertheless do possess a certain status. The doors have bold mouldings and slightly arched tops with dark edgings, and the walls have wooden panelling, even with a bit of faded gold … Likewise clearly visible are dark floorboards, clearly of solid old construction. Yes, what wafts towards us here is the penetrating smell of carbolineum characteristic of public buildings in old East Germany, also found in the West in post-war youth hostels, mixed with the aroma of four-fruit jam.

These wrapped-up pictures continue throughout the rooms, one after the other. They are the only furnishings. It is very likely not only the floor that emits the ominous smell of civil service hygiene's categorical imperative: what immediately also suggests it is the fastidious absence of any content, yes, of any visible substance, which also unexpectedly greeted me on my first visit to the department of historical monuments in East Berlin. On broad stairways and long corridors where it was as if the daylight had to wait outside. But there the stairways and corridors were empty, as if nothing was of importance. Nothing but this smell?

And here? Is it about anything? These blank sheets of paper say nothing. They are nothing like the wrapping Christo lovingly dedicated to something that was special to him. The pictures, presumably once visible, are hidden away behind sandwich paper, without any kind of markings.

einmal sichtbaren Bilder sind weggesteckt hinter dem Butterbrotpapier, ohne Markierungen oder andere Spuren. Selbst ihre tadellosen Anordnungen lassen kein Vorher und kein Nachher vermuten. Was für eine Quarantäne kann das sein? Wenn man genau hinsieht, sind alle Stücke mit einer winzigen Registernummer versehen ...

Man hat es gehört und eben gesagt bekommen: das Zimmer der Hunde. Daran gedacht hätte ich nie. Waren sie denn nicht einfach immer um den alten Fritz, seit seinen jungen Jahren? Als er noch nicht „seinem Staat gedient" hatte, um seinen Untertanen „der Fritz" zu heißen?
Also das Hundezimmer. Ein prachtvoller Kamin aus grauem Marmor. Die Rückwand der einstigen Feuerstelle füllt eine sehr große, kunstvoll gegossene Platte aus dem üblichen Gusseisen aus. Die schräg sich öffnenden Seitenwände prangen in weißen Kacheln mit zart verbundenen Motiven im Delfter Blau, wie es sich gehört. Auch die Windspiele, so schlank, dass man auf allen Bildern die Rippen zählen kann, sollten sich wärmen. Aber man wundert sich doch über den Spiegel, der in fast der ganzen Breite des Kaminsimses bis zu einer Decke geht, die man hoch vermuten muss. Seitlich ist, bis zu den Kanten der nächsten Wände, die im schrägen Winkel den Raum öffnen, nur so wenig Abstand, dass die elegant ausladenden Arme der Bronzeleuchter ihr Gold über die ebenso reich geschnitzten Spiegelrahmen strecken. Sie leben nur noch zum Teil unmittelbar im Tageslicht, das von dem großen Fenster an der rechten, nicht ins Bild geholten Wand des Salons kommt.
Ja, Salon. Das Empfangszimmer für die Hunde des König. Besuchte er denn hier seine Windspiele, die geliebten? Trennte er sich denn je von ihnen? Im Licht dieses Fensters und vor der Öffnung dieser Feuerstelle hat man das Gefühl, hier müsse der wärmste Platz des ganzen Schlosses gewesen sein. So hell und so warm, dass für den Raum Möbel gar nicht nötig waren und das gedeckte Gelb der Wände ausreichte. Wer hätte hier auf Stühlen auch sitzen sollen? Friedrich kam in Wirklichkeit wohl kaum hierher. Und doch ist den Empfangssalon seiner Hunde zu betreten der erste Moment überhaupt, wo man dem Leben der frühen Zeit zu begegnen meint. Jenen Situationen kommt man ohnehin nur in Gedanken näher. Zu greifen sind sie in keinem Detail.

In eines der Möbellager hat es sich zurückgezogen. Das Pathos. Weiße Tücher sind seine Gefährten. Sie eilen ihm wahrscheinlich voraus. Manchmal kommen sie zu früh. Oder sie machen zu viel Wind, zum Beispiel dort, wo sie um einen Kronleuchter geschlagen sind, der so im Fluge ist, dass man ihn schon, weiß umkleidet, davonsegeln sieht. Hier ruht eine schmale Bahn breit hin in leichtem Bogen. Die obere Kante behauptet sich wie die eines eleganten Kanapees darunter. Drei weite Falten und ein scharfer Kniff wehen von ihr über das Schwarz, das von nichts als von Schatten ohne Ende zu sprechen vermag. Dahinter schwingt sich hell ein zweites Tuch bis über eine schmale Kante empor, wie sie eine hölzerne Sessellehne bereitgestellt haben mag. Zwei tiefere Falten helfen den Schatten, die seitlich den Aufschwung begleiten, diesen Elan zu verteilen. Und da, auf der anderen Seite, reckt sich das Dunkel zu einer Kurve empor, der offensichtlich eine Sofalehne ihre Kontur leiht, seitlich von zwei scharfen Schatten zusammengefasst. Sie geben dem Ganzen bereits einen ersten dramatischen Akzent.
Aber was hat das Pathos eingeladen, sich hier niederzulassen? In anderen Räumen breitet sich von den weißen Hussen und Bedeckungen eher Melancholie aus. Manchmal empfinden wir sie

Even their immaculate arrangements tell us nothing about before and after. What kind of quarantine can that be? When one looks very closely, one sees that all the wrappings are marked with a tiny registration number …

One has just heard it being said: 'The Dogs' Room'. I would never have thought it. Weren't the dogs always with 'old Fritz', even in his youth? Even before he had 'served his state' and come to be called 'Fritz' by his subjects?

So: The Dogs' Room. A magnificent grey marble fireplace. At the back is a very large and elaborate fireback in the usual cast iron. The oblique side walls bear white tiles decorated with delicately joined-up motifs in Delft blue, as is fitting. The greyhounds – which in all the pictures are so slim that one can count their ribs – also had to be able to warm themselves. Somewhat surprising, however, is the mirror above, which is almost as broad as the mantelpiece and extends up to what is presumably a high ceiling. To the side, going along to obtuse-angled corners that open up the space, there is only just enough room for the elegantly extended arms of the bronze chandelier to stretch their gold over the likewise richly carved mirror frame. They already no longer live directly in the light that streams in through the large window in the drawing room's right-hand wall beyond the edge of the image.

Yes, drawing room. The king's dogs' reception room. Was it here, then, that he visited his beloved greyhounds? Was he ever in fact separated from them? Standing in the light from the window and in front of the hearth, one feels that this must have been the warmest spot in the whole palace. So bright and so warm that there was no need for furniture and the muted yellow of the walls sufficed. And who would have sat on chairs here? Frederick very likely hardly ever came here himself. Yet entering his dogs' reception room gives one, for the very first time, a feeling of actually encountering the life of times past. Anyway, one only comes closer to those situations in thought. There are no details that allow them to be grasped.

It has withdrawn to one of the furniture depots. Pathos. White cloths are its companions. They probably hurry on ahead. Sometimes they even get there too early. Or they flap around too much, getting wrapped around a chandelier, for example, which has so much wind in its sails that it seems about to fly away, all clad in white. Here a slender length of cloth is stretched out along the floor in a slight curve, the upper edge posturing like the outline of an elegant couch below. Three further folds and a sharp crease drift away from it over the black, which cannot speak of anything but shadows without end. Behind, a second cloth swings brightly upwards over a narrow ledge, just as it might have done on the back of a wooden chair. Two deeper folds help the shadows, which accompany the upswing to the side, to distribute this momentum. And there, on the other side, the darkness rises to form a curve, which obviously gets its outline from a sofa back, flanked by two sharp shadows. They give the whole scene a first dramatic accent.

But what prompted pathos to make its home here in the first place? In other rooms, not pathos but melancholy emanates from the white furniture coverings. Sometimes we even feel them to be liberating, freeing us from burdensomely official presences. What here can assist heroic resignation in pushing on through to the end? From under the lengths of cloth and over them and

auch geradezu als eine Befreiung von lästig offizieller Präsenz. Was hilft hier denn doch einer heroischen Resignation, alles zu durchziehen? Von unter den Leinenbahnen und über sie hin, aus Winkeln und in die Ecken? Schmale schwergraue Balken recken sich aus der Unterwelt des Raumes empor wie die Beine umgedrehter Tische. Doch gerade und bis zur Decke, mit einer Querstrebe für den Halt. Eine Tapete mit blassgrauen Mustern schließt nach hinten die Kammer ab und macht zugleich die Wand durchlässig für die Stimmung des Verwehens. Ihre kaum wahrnehmbaren Muster sind wie die Fußspuren vor sehr Langem hier durchgeeilter Erinyen. Scharf dagegen die Schattenkante einer übergroßen Kartonfläche. Weiß, als sei ein Tuch aufrechtstehend gegen die Wand gefroren. Nach oben verdämmert es im Vergessen des unten auf Bahnen hervortretenden Lichts, das sich aber auch da an Beugen und geknitterten Grübchen und schließlich im Sog unergründlicher Zwischenräume verliert.

Eine Gegend des Schlosses hat sich mit Beige und Hellgrau begnügt, auf die Wand und das Holz der Tür und ihren Sockel verteilt. Wo mag sie sich befinden? Immerhin hat sie Profile und Bogen. Also vermutlich Umfeld eines besseren Quartiers. Das Beige ist düster braun eingerahmt, in der Ecke, oben und unten. Möbel keine, Bilder keine. Also eher Flur, nicht einmal Vorzimmer. Doch man hat der Wand zwischen Tür und Ecke einmal eine Funktion zugewiesen.
Zwei Reihen Geweihe sind hier gelandet, wie ein kleiner Schof Enten. Eine verstaubte Improvisation. Nicht sehr eindrucksvolle Schaufeln von Damwild, eigentlich zierlich. Zierlich macht für eine Sammlung von Jagdtrophäen nicht viel her. Aber beseitigen wollte man sie auch nicht. Auch nicht zu jenen Kronleuchtern verarbeiten, die in alten Häusern als fliegende Friedhöfe getäfelte Hallen und Herrenzimmer auszeichnen. Stolz ist niemand auf sie gewesen. Statt auf Wappenschilde aus Eichenholz aufgesetzt zu sein, sind sie mit dem Stück Kopf des Wildes zwischen den Ansätzen des Geweihs auf einem kleinen Stück Brett befestigt. So sind diese, ungebeizt und leicht schief, mal nach rechts und mal nach links, ihrerseits auf zwei Leisten aufgesetzt, die von der Decke bis auf den Hauptteil der Wand reichen. Am unteren Ende der einen fristet, mit ein wenig mehr Abstand, ein winziger Rest eines Rehbocks eine prekäre Existenz. Der Jäger nennt so etwas einen Spießer, zu Recht.
Also, man hat Vorkehrungen für ihr Bleiben getroffen, ohne Wert darauf zu legen. Man sieht, es hatte schon eine Berechtigung, dass auf Hofjagden den Herrschaften nur Prachtexemplare zugetrieben wurden. Trophäen erlegten Wildes, die sich nicht zum Triumphieren eignen, hinterlassen nur Peinlichkeit. Wo lässt man sie? Zwischen dem Jagdzimmer mit großen Porträts der Jäger und der freien Wand neben der Besenkammer? Doch bietet diese nicht sehr berühmte Ecke den verwaisten Knochen eine gut gepflegte Station zwischen königlichen, vielleicht schon kaiserlichen Forsten und nirgendwo. Die Spur zum Leben später Prinzen des Preußenhauses gelte es zu verfolgen.

Was fliegt denn da? Ein Schwarm kleiner weißer Tupfer, nein, schon Rechtecke verschiedener Form verteilt sich über eine Tapete in blassen Farben. Fast quadratisch manche, andere länglich. In dichteren Haufen oder ganz allein. Ihre Kanten stehen parallel und im rechten Winkel zu dem Sims des Raumes, das oben über dem Rand der Tapete dem Bild einen würdigen Abschluss gibt. Die letzten des Schwarms drängen sich gegen seine untere Kante, durchsichtiger als die

away, from nooks and crannies and into the corners? Slender dark-grey beams rise upwards from the underworld of the room like the legs of inverted tables. But straight and right up to the ceiling, with a crossbar to hold them fast. The room terminates in a wallpaper with pale grey patterns that make the wall permeable to the atmosphere of drifting away. Its barely perceptible patterns are like the tracks of Furies that hurried through long ago. Contrastingly sharp is the edge of the shadow cast by an oversize panel of cardboard. White, as if a standing sheet had frozen to the wall. Further up it darkens, oblivious to the light shining forward in strips below, which itself also dims on bends and crumpled-up hollows, finally fading out entirely, exhausted by the tow of unfathomable intervening spaces.

One area of the palace has contented itself with beige and pale grey, distributed around the walls and the wood and base of the door. Where might this door be? It does have mouldings and an arched top, so it is presumably near one of the quarters with greater pretensions. The beige is framed with a gloomy brown, in the corner and at top and bottom. Nothing of furniture, of pictures. Most likely a hall or corridor, not even an antechamber. But the wall between the door and the corner was once given a function.

Two rows of antlers have landed here, like a little clutch of ducklings. A fusty improvisation. Not very impressive shovel antlers from fallow deer, rather dainty ones in fact. While daintiness is not exactly an asset in a collection of hunting trophies, they clearly didn't want to get rid of them either. Or to make them into those flying cemetery chandeliers that are typical features of halls and gentlemen's rooms in old houses. But these trophies can never have been a source of pride to anyone. Instead of being mounted on oak shields like coats of arms, they are affixed to little pieces of wood with the piece of bone between the antlers left visible. And the pieces of wood, not even stained, are slightly askew, some listing to the right and some to the left, affixed to two wooden strips stretching down from the ceiling to the main section of the wall. At the lower end of one strip, precariously positioned at a slight distance from its neighbour, is the tiny relic of a roebuck shot in its second year, in shooting parlance a 'pricket'.

So, arrangements were made for them to stay, but without according them much importance. It was clearly not for nothing that only the finest specimens were driven towards the guns at court hunts. Game trophies that give no grounds for triumph are simply an embarrassment. Where does one leave them? Between the hunting room with its large portraits of sportsmen and the vacant wall next to the broom cupboard? This far from celebrated corner at least provides the orphaned bones with a well-cared-for home between royal or perhaps even imperial forests and simply nowhere. Which later prince of the House of Prussia, one wonders, might they be traced back to?

What are those things flying around there? Spreading itself over a pale-coloured wallpaper is a swarm of what look like little white swabs. No, they're all rectangular, some almost square, others elongated. Some in dense groups and some on their own. Their edges are parallel and at right angles to the cornice that runs around the room bringing the image to a worthy end at the top of the wallpaper. The last ones in the flock throng against its lower edge, more transparent than most, though others lining themselves up in long rows or forming clumps are just as pale.

meisten anderen. Nur, wo diese sich zu längeren Streifen reihen oder miteinander verklumpen, sind sie auch ganz blass.

Wo ist der Kasten, aus dem all diese kleinen Pflaster ausgeschwärmt sind? Nein, jedes ist anders geschnitten. Liebevolle Hände müssen sie vorbereitet haben, bevor sie diese Fläche aufsuchen konnten. Vielleicht wurden sie eben doch sorgfältig platziert. Doch es liegt ein ganz leichter grauer Schimmer über ihrem Feld, dem sie in ihrer Durchsichtigkeit verwandt sind. Sie landeten nicht unvorbereitet, nicht irgendwo. Zugleich bilden sie einen Schwarm, derart, dass man den Eindruck hat, sie würden weiterziehen. Und für diese Bewegung haben sie hier einen Anführer gefunden. Auf der Tapete sind groß und farbig, schön und deutlich die Schwingen, der Kopf und der Stoß eines edlen Vogels zu sehen. Die Schwingen mit fein gespreizten Federn. Der Stoß im eleganten Schwung bis in die sehr langen roten Federn der Spitze ausgreifend. Der Kopf zurückgewandt gegen die seitliche Richtung seines Flugs, aber auf diese sehr wohl orientiert durch die kühn sich von ihm aufschwingende kleine Feder an seiner hinteren Rundung.

Dieser Elan ist so schön und so stark, dass man die Empfindung hat, all die weißen Flecken machen sich auf, ihm zu folgen. Auf der Tapete nimmt man nur zwei, drei große Schattenbahnen wahr. Keine Muster, keine anderen Motive halten den Schwarm zurück – bis auf ein verstümmeltes Gebilde, das die Flecken schon überklebt und abgewiesen. Es wird zurückgelassen werden in dem großen, vermutlich aber still schwebenden Aufbruch, dem der paradiesische Vogel mit seinen tiefblauen und hellroten Federn ein schönes Land verspricht. Vielleicht hat er nur auf den Schwarm der weißen Flecken gewartet. Er blickt ja hinter sich, wie um sich ihrer sicher zu sein.

„Petites perceptions" nennt Leibniz alle unsere Wahrnehmungen, die bei der unbewussten Aufnahme bestimmter Atmosphären beginnen und unser Bewusstsein bis in transzendente Gewissheiten begleiten. Er sah darin eine Parallele zu seiner Erfindung der Infinitesimalrechnung.

Where is the box that all these little plasters have swarmed out of? But no, every one is cut differently. They must have been prepared with loving hands before they were able to find their way to this surface. Or perhaps they were very carefully placed there. But over their field lies a very light grey shimmer to which they are related in their transparency. They did not land unprepared or just anywhere. At the same time the way in which they form a flock gives the impression that they would gladly fly onwards. And for this they have found a leader. Depicted large and clear in colour on the wallpaper are the wings, tail feathers, and head of a noble bird. The wings with the primaries finely splayed out; the tail with an elegant sense of movement right down to the very long red feathers at the end; and the head turned away from its sideways flight, but still oriented towards it, as is clear from the small feathers turned boldly upwards at its rounded rump.
The great bird is moving with such fine, strong elan that all the white patches seem to be making a move to follow it. Only two or three large swathes can be made out upon the wallpaper. No patterns, no other motifs hold the flock of patches back – except for a mutilated shape dismissively stuck over them. It will be left behind in the grand but presumably silent soaring departure which for the paradisiac bird with its deep-blue and scarlet feathers holds out the promise of a beautiful land. Maybe the grand bird had just been waiting for the flock of white patches. After all, it is looking back, as if to be sure of them.

'Petites perceptions' was Leibniz's term for all perceptions that start with our unconscious sensing of certain atmospheres and accompany our consciousness even as far as transcendental certainties. He saw a parallel between this process and the infinitesimal calculus that he invented.

МЕРТЬ НЕМЕЦКИМ
ЗАХВАТЧИКАМ!

POTSDAM

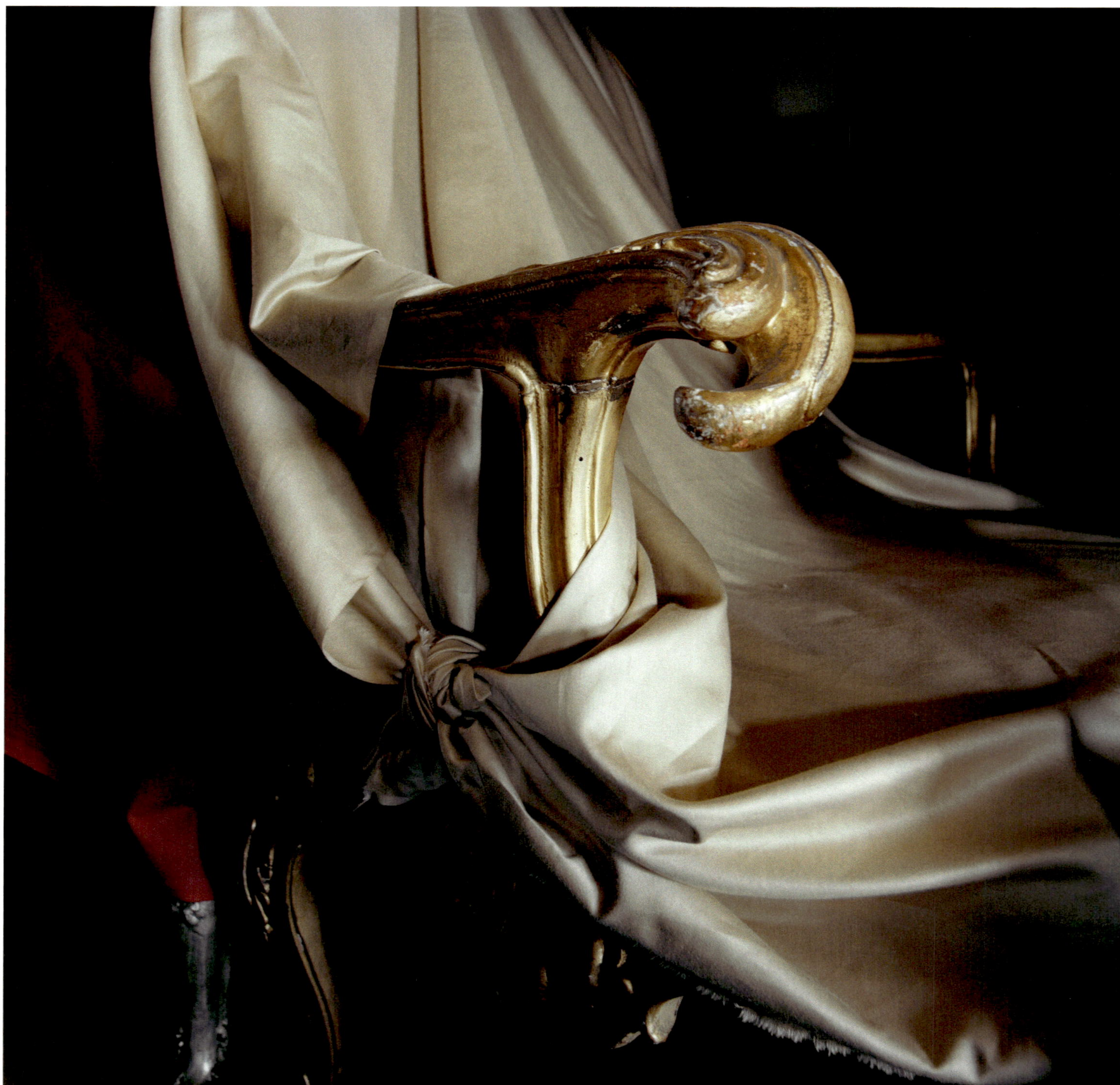

12499
3533

WO DIE AUFNAHMEN ENTSTANDEN

Bei ihren Besuchen im Neuen Palais erhielt Friederike von Rauch freien Zugang zu nahezu allen Bereichen. Es ging nicht darum, alle Räume des Schlosses dokumentarisch zu erfassen. Die Auswahl der Bilder erfolgte ebenso nicht in der Absicht einer gleichmäßigen Vollständigkeit der Verteilung oder eines Rundgangs. Die roten Nummern in den Grundrissen kennzeichnen die Seitenzahlen der Aufnahmen, die im jeweiligen Raum entstanden sind.

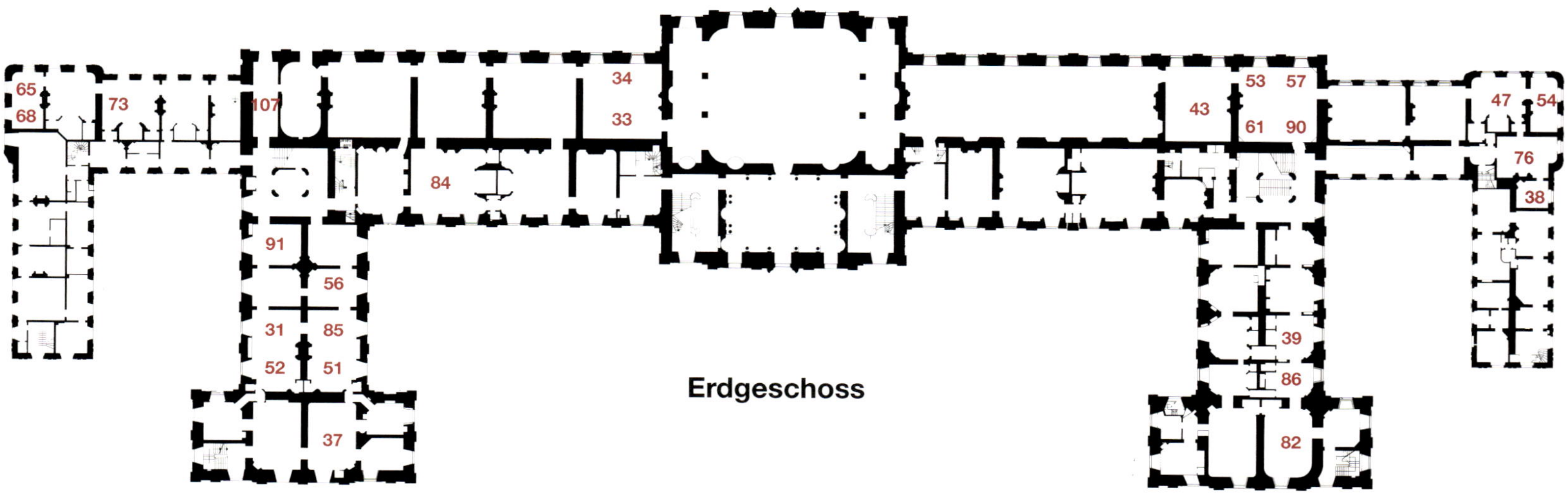


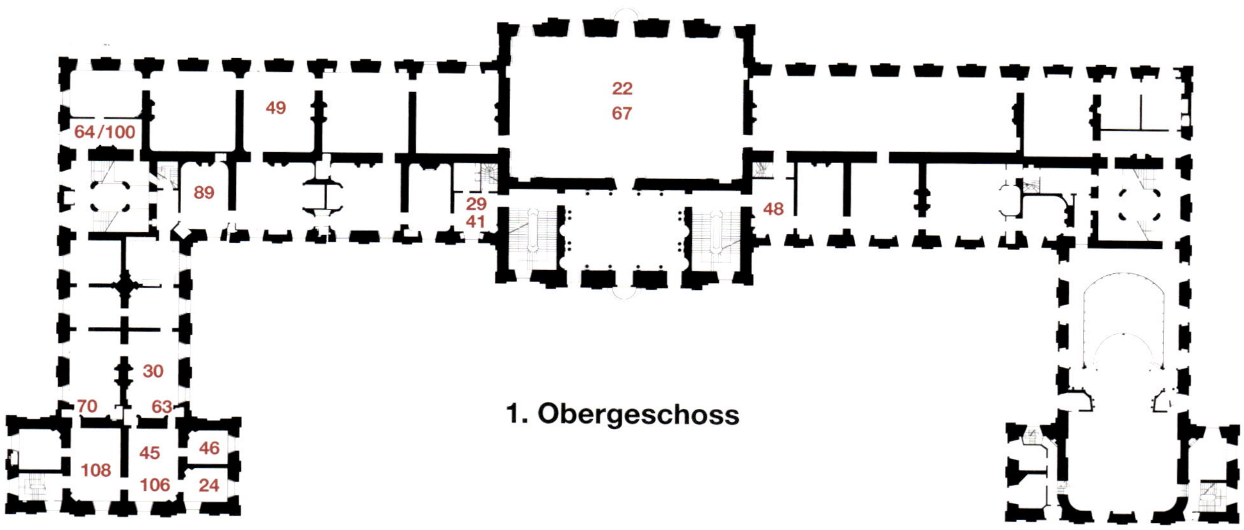

WHERE THE PHOTOGRAPHS WERE TAKEN

On her visits to the New Palace, Friederike von Rauch was allowed access to almost all areas of the building. Free from any obligation to make a documentary record of every single room. Similarly, the pictures were not selected with a view to having all parts of the palace represented equally or to simulating a guided tour. The red numbers on the floor plans relate to the pages bearing photographs taken at the respective location.

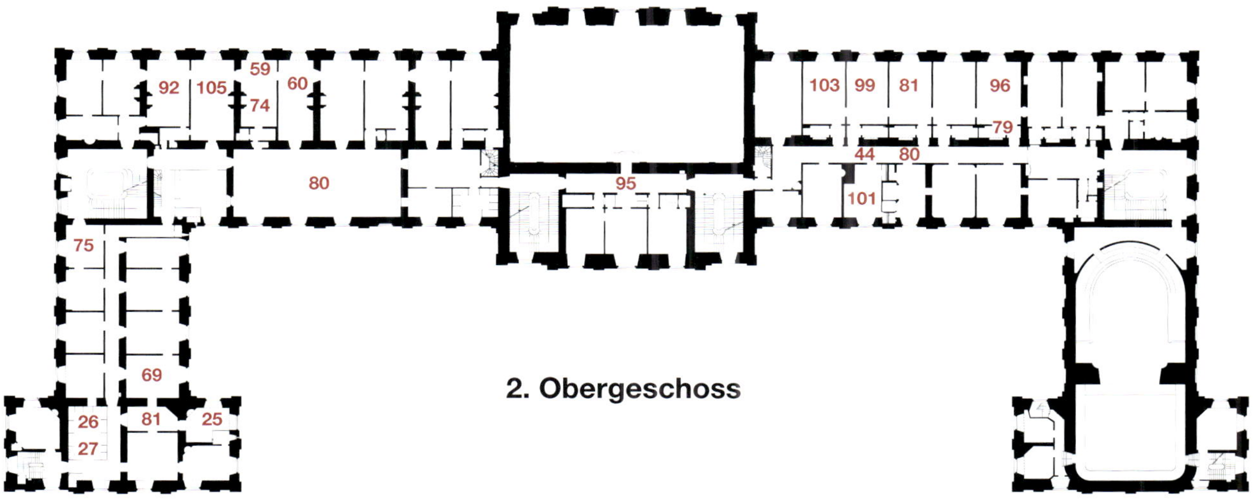


2. Obergeschoss

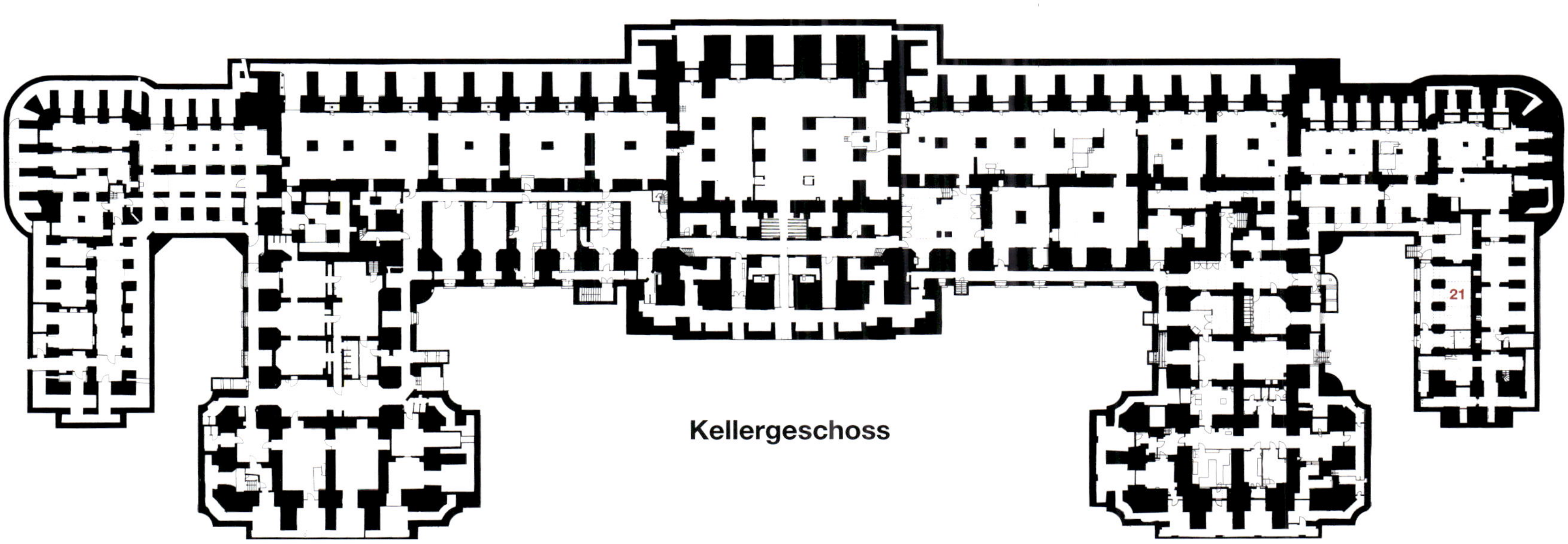


Kellergeschoss

Dieses Buch ist allen Mitarbeiterinnen und Mitarbeitern aus den Bereichen der Depotverwaltung, der Graphischen Sammlungen, der Restaurierung und der Schlossbereichsleitung gewidmet, denen das Neue Palais ein vertrauter Arbeitsort war und ist.

This book is dedicated to all staff members of the Depositories Administration Office, the Collection of Prints and Drawings, the Restoration Department and the Palace Management, for whom the New Palace was and is a familiar place of work.



Umschlagmotiv | Cover: Friederike von Rauch

Lektorat (Deutsch) | Copy Editor (German): Ute Rummel, Kairo
Übersetzung | Translation: John Nicholson
Gestaltung und Satz | Design and setting: Susanne Rösler, jovis
Lithografie | Lithography: Carsten Humme, Leipzig
Druck und Bindung | Printing and Binding: Grafisches Centrum Cuno, Calbe

Bibliografische Information der Deutschen Nationalbibliothek
Die Deutsche Nationalbibliothek verzeichnet diese Publikation in der Deutschen Nationalbibliografie; detaillierte bibliografische Daten sind im Internet über http://dnb.d-nb.de abrufbar.
Bibliographic information published by the Deutsche Nationalbibliothek
The Deutsche Nationalbibliothek lists this publication in the Deutsche Nationalbibliografie; detailed bibliographic data are available on the Internet at http://dnb.d-nb.de

jovis Verlag GmbH
Kurfürstenstraße 15/16
10785 Berlin

www.jovis.de

jovis-Bücher sind weltweit im ausgewählten Buchhandel erhältlich. Informationen zu unserem internationalen Vertrieb erhalten Sie von Ihrem Buchhändler oder unter www.jovis.de.
jovis books are available worldwide in select bookstores. Please contact your nearest bookseller or visit www.jovis.de for information concerning your local distribution.

ISBN 978-3-86859-549-9